A GIFT FOR:

....

FROM:

....

Published by Hallmark Gift Books,
a division of Hallmark Cards, Inc.,
Kansas City, MO 64141
Visit us on the Web at Hallmark.com.

Editorial Director: Delia Berrigan
Writer and Editor: Megan Langford
Art Director: Jan Mastin
Designer: Mark Voss
Lettering Artist: Sarah Cole
Production Designer: Dan Horton

ISBN: 978-1-59530-586-2
BOK1252

Made in China

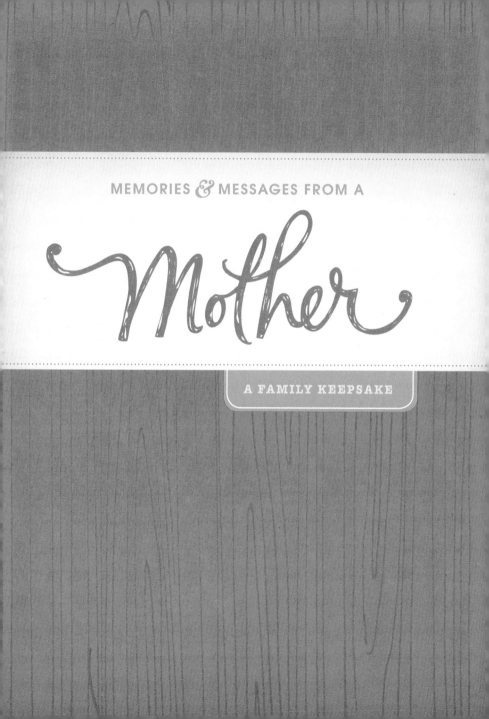

MEMORIES & MESSAGES FROM A

Mother

A FAMILY KEEPSAKE

CONTENTS

Dear ....,

We've had countless conversations, but there are still
many stories I've never told you. Life keeps us busy,
and I don't always take the time to sit down and talk
about myself. I am giving you this book so you can read
about those stories and always remember them. After all,
by learning about my childhood, my education—even
my hobbies and role models—you'll understand how
I became the person—and the mother—I am today.

Nothing in this world is as important as family, and I
hope that reading this book will give you a better under-
standing of where you come from. Whether they make
you laugh or bring you to tears, may the memories and
messages I've written here bring us closer together.

Love,

....

*Good women and mothers
aren't born with all the answers.
It's something they grow into,
experience by experience,
choice by choice, and not without
a few mistakes along the way.*

MY FULL NAME IS:

....

MY FRIENDS CALL ME:

....

MY BIRTHDAY IS:

....

AS I WRITE THIS, I AM:

 **YEARS OLD**

MY CHILDHOOD
NICKNAME WAS:

....

BECAUSE:

....

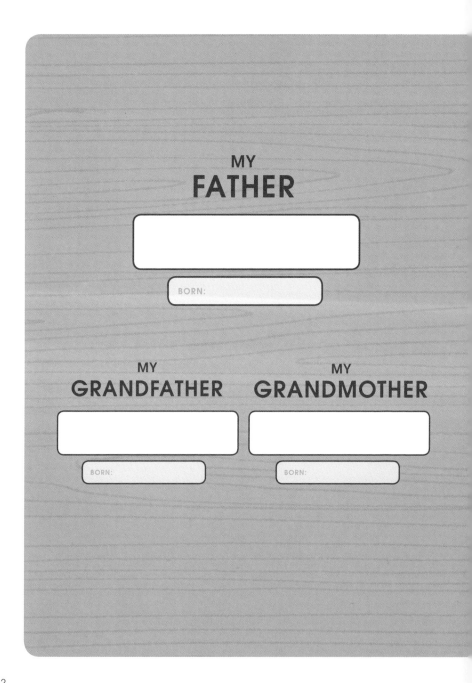

MY
FATHER

BORN:

MY
GRANDFATHER

MY
GRANDMOTHER

BORN:

BORN:

MY
MOTHER

BORN:

MY
GRANDFATHER

BORN:

MY
GRANDMOTHER

BORN:

MY DAD'S JOB:

....

....

MY MOM'S JOB:

....

....

A STORY ABOUT MY PARENTS
THAT I NEVER GET TIRED OF TELLING IS:

....

....

....

....

....

....

....

EVERYBODY CALLS HER GRANDPARENTS SOMETHING DIFFERENT.

HERE ARE THE NAMES FOR MINE:

ONE THING
YOU SHOULD KNOW ABOUT
MY GRANDPARENTS:

I WAS BORN IN:

....

AND GREW UP IN:

....

OUR HOME LOOKED LIKE:

....

....

....

....

THESE ARE THE PEOPLE I LIVED WITH:

....

....

....

....

PEOPLE SAID I LOOKED JUST LIKE:

....

I ALWAYS THOUGHT I LOOKED LIKE:

....

A PERSON I ALWAYS
LOOKED UP TO WAS:

....

....

....

....

....

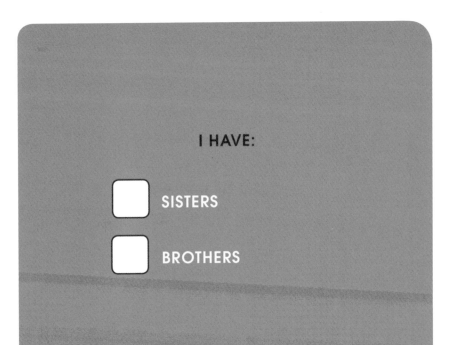

I HAVE:

☐ SISTERS

☐ BROTHERS

I AM:

☐ OLDEST
☐ IN THE MIDDLE
☐ YOUNGEST

MY SIBLINGS AND I SPENT HOURS:

....

....

....

....

....

....

....

MY FIRST BEST FRIEND'S NAME WAS:

....

HERE'S HOW WE MET:

....

....

....

....

....

....

MY THREE MOST-LOVED
CHILDHOOD TOYS:

1. ....

2. ....

3. ....

ONE OF MY FAVORITE EARLY MEMORIES IS:

WHEN I WAS A KID,
ONE OF MY FAVORITE THINGS TO DO WAS:

EVERYONE THOUGHT
I WAS REALLY GOOD AT:

....

....

....

....

....

HERE IS SOMETHING THAT WAS DIFFICULT FOR ME AS A CHILD:

....

....

....

....

I ALWAYS WISHED I WAS BETTER AT:

HERE'S HOW I EARNED MONEY AS A KID:

....

....

HERE'S HOW I SPENT IT:

....

....

WHEN I WAS LITTLE,
I WANTED TO GROW UP TO BECOME A:

....

....

....

....

....

....

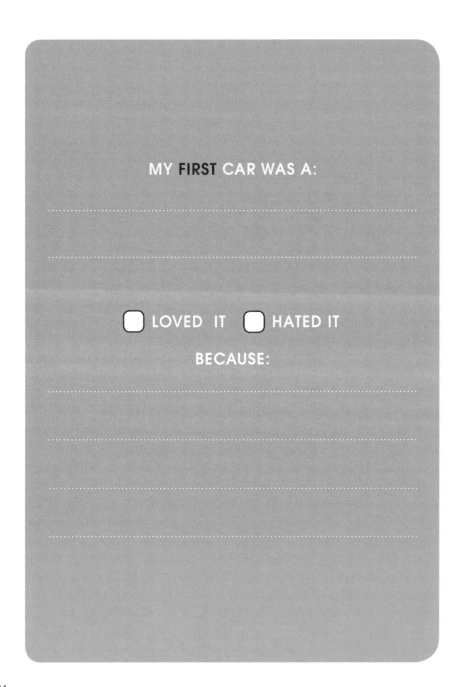

MY FIRST CAR WAS A:

....

....

☐ LOVED IT ☐ HATED IT

BECAUSE:

....

....

....

....

THE **BEST PLACE** THAT CAR EVER TOOK ME WAS:

....

....

....

....

STYLES MAY CHANGE,
BUT MY FAVORITE OUTFIT
OF ALL TIME WAS:

....

....

....

IF I COULD HAVE KEPT
ONE HAIRDO
FOR THE REST OF MY LIFE,
IT WOULD HAVE BEEN:

....

....

....

....

....

SOME OF MY CHILDHOOD FAVORITE FOODS WERE:

- ☐ CHEESEBURGERS
- ☐ MEAT LOAF
- ☐ PIZZA
- ☐ MACARONI AND CHEESE
- ☐ SPAGHETTI
- ☐ FISH STICKS
- ☐ ....
- ☐ ....
- ☐ ....

ONE MEAL I WILL NEVER FORGET IS:

....

....

WHEN I WAS LITTLE,
MY FAMILY DESCRIBED ME AS:

- ⬜ SWEET
- ⬜ KIND
- ⬜ ADVENTUROUS
- ⬜ LOVING
- ⬜ CARING
- ⬜ LOUD
- ⬜ FUNNY
- ⬜ ATHLETIC
- ⬜ SHY
- ⬜ OUTGOING
- ⬜ ....
- ⬜ ....
- ⬜ ....

WHEN I WAS GROWING UP, I BELIEVED:

....

....

....

....

....

AS AN ADULT, I BELIEVE:

....

....

....

....

....

Somewhere along the way it just happens—we learn to trust ourselves, and we grow strong enough to take risks and smart enough to know which ones to take. And then one day we realize that little by little, we're becoming the people we were meant to be all along.

Education

I ATTENDED ELEMENTARY SCHOOL AT:

....

TO GET THERE, I:

☐ WALKED

☐ TOOK THE BUS

☐ RODE MY BIKE

☐ RODE IN A CAR

☐ ....

ONE REALLY FUNNY STORY ABOUT
ELEMENTARY SCHOOL:

....

....

....

....

....

....

NOBODY SEEMS TO LOVE MIDDLE SCHOOL, BUT FOR ME, THE WORST PART WAS:

....

....

....

....

THE BEST PART WAS:

....

....

....

....

....

IN HIGH SCHOOL,
MY FAVORITE CLASSES WERE:

....

....

....

HERE ARE A FEW EXTRACURRICULAR
ACTIVITIES I PARTICIPATED IN:

....

....

....

MY GRADES WERE:

☐ NOT SO GOOD

☐ GOOD

☐ VERY GOOD

☐ EXCELLENT

FOR FUN, I LIKED TO:

- ☐ GO TO CONCERTS
- ☐ SEE MOVIES
- ☐ GO TO PARTIES
- ☐ PLAY SPORTS
- ☐ ....
- ☐ ....
- ☐ ....

HERE ARE SOME UNFORGETTABLE THINGS FROM THAT TIME:

MOVIES: ....

....

SONGS: ....

....

POLITICAL EVENTS: ....

....

FASHION TRENDS: ....

....

MY BEST FRIENDS WERE:

....

....

....

THE TEACHER
WHO MOST INFLUENCED ME WAS:

....

BECAUSE:

....

....

....

....

....

AFTER HIGH SCHOOL, I WANTED TO:

....

....

....

HERE'S WHAT I ACTUALLY DID
AFTER HIGH SCHOOL:

☐ MOVED AWAY FROM HOME

☐ WENT TO COLLEGE

☐ WENT TO TRADE SCHOOL

☐ PURSUED A CAREER

☐ ....

THOSE FIRST FEW YEARS
AFTER HIGH SCHOOL WERE:

....

....

....

....

....

MY COLLEGE YEARS WERE SPENT:

THREE PEOPLE
I MET IN COLLEGE WHOM I'LL NEVER FORGET:

1. ....

2. ....

3. ....

I CHANGED MY MAJOR ☐ TIMES
AND FINALLY DECIDED TO STUDY:

....

IN THE END, I:

☐ EARNED A DEGREE IN ....

☐ GRADUATED EARLY

☐ TOOK EXTRA SEMESTERS TO FINISH SCHOOL

☐ NEVER GRADUATED

☐ ....

HERE'S HOW MY EDUCATION INFLUENCED WHERE I AM TODAY:

....

....

....

....

....

....

....

I'D LIKE TO LEARN MORE ABOUT:

....

....

....

....

....

....

....

*Every successful career is marked
by the contributions and
accomplishments made by an
individual, both big and small.*

Working Hard

MY FIRST JOB WAS:

....

....

WHEN I FIRST STARTED WORKING, I FELT:

....

....

....

MY CURRENT JOB IS:

....

....

I'D DESCRIBE IT AS:

....

....

....

HERE ARE THREE THINGS
I LOVE ABOUT WHAT I DO:

....

....

....

**HERE ARE THREE THINGS I WISH
I COULD CHANGE ABOUT WHAT I DO:**

....

....

....

IF I COULD START MY CAREER
ALL OVER AGAIN, I WOULD:

....

....

....

....

....

....

IF I COULD DO ANYTHING
IN THE WORLD, I WOULD:

....

....

....

THE WORST BOSS
I EVER HAD TAUGHT ME:

....

....

....

....

....

....

THE BEST BOSS
I EVER HAD TAUGHT ME:

....

....

....

....

....

....

❁

MY COWORKERS DESCRIBE ME AS:

- ☐ TRUSTWORTHY
- ☐ HARDWORKING
- ☐ PERPETUALLY LATE
- ☐ PUNCTUAL
- ☐ FUNNY
- ☐ QUIET
- ☐ SMART
- ☐ STRONG
- ☐ DETAIL-ORIENTED
- ☐ ....

I THINK MY BEST QUALITIES
AS AN EMPLOYEE ARE:

....

....

....

....

....

....

*There is nowhere
you can go where
love can't follow.*

I FIRST FELL IN LOVE
WHEN I WAS:

....

I'LL NEVER FORGET:

....

....

MY FIRST KISS WAS WITH:

....

I'D DESCRIBE IT AS:

◯ ROMANTIC

◯ AWKWARD

◯ GROSS

◯ FUNNY

◯ ....

◯ ....

◯ ....

HERE'S THE STORY OF
HOW I MET YOUR FATHER:

THREE THINGS
THAT FIRST ATTRACTED ME TO HIM:

1. ....

2. ....

3. ....

TO ME, LOVE IS:

....

....

....

....

....

....

....

SOMETIMES, LOVE ISN'T EASY.
ONE THING I'VE LEARNED IS:

I GOT MARRIED ON ....

IN ....

THREE THINGS
I REMEMBER MOST ABOUT
MY WEDDING DAY:

1. ....

2. ....

3. ....

TO ME, MARRIAGE IS ALL ABOUT:

....

....

....

....

....

....

....

....

....

BEFORE I GOT MARRIED, **I NEVER THOUGHT:**

....

....

....

....

....

....

....

MY MARRIAGE IS:

- [ ] A PARTNERSHIP
- [ ] FULL OF GIVE-AND-TAKE
- [ ] SOLID
- [ ] ROCKY AT TIMES
- [ ] FUN
- [ ] FULL OF ROMANCE
- [ ] ....
- [ ] ....
- [ ] ....

HERE ARE SOME OF THE WAYS WE HAVE
CELEBRATED OUR ANNIVERSARY:

ONE OF MY
FAVORITE DATES WAS:

....

....

....

....

....

MY FAVORITE LOVE SONG IS:

....

....

....

IF MY LOVE LIFE
WERE A MOVIE, IT WOULD BE:

- ☐ A DRAMA WITH LOTS OF UPS AND DOWNS

- ☐ A LAUGHED-SO-HARD-WE-CRIED COMEDY

- ☐ A ROMANTIC COMEDY WITH A PERFECT, HAPPILY-EVER-AFTER ENDING

- ☐ ....

IF I COULD TEACH YOU ONLY
ONE THING
ABOUT LOVE, IT WOULD BE:

....

....

....

....

Being family is more than sharing the same genes and family history. Being family means knowing when to give hugs, knowing when to give space, and most important, knowing when to stick together.

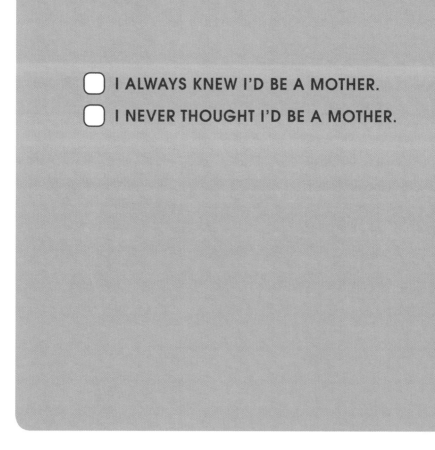

☐ I ALWAYS KNEW I'D BE A MOTHER.

☐ I NEVER THOUGHT I'D BE A MOTHER.

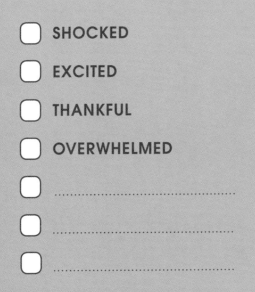

WHEN I FOUND OUT
I WAS GOING TO BE A MOM,
I WAS:

- ☐ SHOCKED
- ☐ EXCITED
- ☐ THANKFUL
- ☐ OVERWHELMED
- ☐ ....
- ☐ ....
- ☐ ....

THE FIRST TIME I HELD YOU IN MY ARMS, I FELT:

....

....

....

....

....

....

....

WHEN I BECAME A MOTHER, MY LIFE
CHANGED FOREVER. HERE'S WHY:

....

....

....

....

....

....

....

....

OVER THE YEARS, I'VE LEARNED A LOT
ABOUT BEING A MOM. WHEN I FIRST
BECAME A MOTHER, HERE ARE SOME
THINGS I WISH I'D KNOWN:

THE PARENTING MOMENT
I AM MOST PROUD OF IS:

....

....

....

....

....

....

RAISING A FAMILY IS:

- ☐ AMAZING
- ☐ CHALLENGING
- ☐ UNBELIEVABLE
- ☐ MY GREATEST ACHIEVEMENT
- ☐ ....
- ☐ ....
- ☐ ....

ONE OF MY FAVORITE
FAMILY MEMORIES IS:

MY MOST-LOVED FAMILY TRADITION IS:

DURING YOUR CHILDHOOD, WHEN WE WANTED TO DO SOMETHING SPECIAL TOGETHER AS A FAMILY, WE WOULD:

....

....

....

....

HERE'S WHAT A TYPICAL DAY WAS LIKE FOR US WHEN YOU WERE LITTLE:

....

....

....

....

AT OUR HOUSE, BIRTHDAYS WERE:

☐ HUGE CELEBRATIONS

☐ NOT A BIG DEAL

☐ CELEBRATED WITH CAKE AND PRESENTS

☐ THE MOST FUN DAYS OF THE YEAR

☐ ....

☐ ....

☐ ....

THE BEST BIRTHDAY GIFT
I EVER RECEIVED WAS:

....

....

....

THE HOLIDAY I MOST LOOK FORWARD TO IS:

....

BECAUSE:

....

....

....

....

ON THAT DAY, WE ALWAYS:

....

....

....

....

....

....

I'M SO GLAD YOU TAUGHT ME TO:

....

....

....

....

....

....

....

....

HERE ARE SOME THINGS I HOPE
YOU'VE LEARNED FROM ME:

☐ HOW TO TIE YOUR SHOES

☐ TO ALWAYS SAY "PLEASE"
AND "THANK YOU"

☐ TO BE KIND

☐ WHICH FORK TO USE FIRST

☐ ....

☐ ....

☐ ....

I'LL NEVER FORGET THE DAY YOU TOLD ME:

....

....

....

....

....

....

....

A MOTHER CAN'T HELP BUT GIVE ADVICE TO HER CHILDREN.
HERE'S MY ADVICE FOR YOU:

OUR FAMILY VACATIONS WERE:

☐ NOISY

☐ BUSY

☐ RELAXING

☐ FUN

☐ SIMPLE

☐ ....

☐ ....

☐ ....

MY FAVORITE PLACE TO GO WAS:

☐ THE BEACH

☐ THE MOUNTAINS

☐ CAMPING

☐ OVERSEAS

☐ HISTORIC SITES

☐ ON A ROAD TRIP

☐ ....

☐ ....

THINGS JUST WOULDN'T BE
THE SAME WITHOUT PETS.
HERE'S A FAVORITE STORY ABOUT OURS:

....

....

....

....

....

....

....

....

THREE THINGS
I LEARNED FROM OUR PET:

1. ....

2. ....

3. ....

*You have to color outside the
lines once in a while if you want
to make your life a masterpiece.*

More About Me

HERE ARE A FEW OF MY
FAVORITE THINGS:

MOVIE: ....

SONG: ....

SPORT: ....

SPORTS TEAM: ....

FOOD: ....

TV SHOW: ....

VACATION SPOT: ....

BOOK: ....

AFTER A LONG DAY, HERE'S HOW I LIKE TO RELAX AND UNWIND:

....

....

....

....

....

....

....

....

IF THERE WERE ONE CATCHPHRASE
I'D LIKE TO BE KNOWN FOR, IT WOULD BE:

....

....

....

....

MY PERSONAL PHILOSOPHY IS:

....

....

....

....

....

....

....

A FEW OF MY HOBBIES ARE:

- ☐ READING
- ☐ BICYCLING
- ☐ BAKING
- ☐ CRAFTING
- ☐ KNITTING
- ☐ GARDENING
- ☐ GOLFING
- ☐ ....
- ☐ ....
- ☐ ....
- ☐ ....

IN MY FREE TIME, I LOVE TO:

....

....

....

....

....

....

....

_____ **MAKES ME FEEL BEAUTIFUL.**

I NEVER LEAVE THE HOUSE WITHOUT MY:

WHEN I SHOP, I USUALLY BUY:

- ☐ GROCERIES
- ☐ CLOTHES
- ☐ A NEW PURSE
- ☐ THINGS FOR MY FAMILY
- ☐ JEWELRY
- ☐ BOOKS
- ☐ ....
- ☐ ....
- ☐ ....

THREE THINGS
THAT ALWAYS INSPIRE ME ARE:

1. ....

2. ....

3. ....

AN INCREDIBLY INFLUENTIAL PERSON
IN MY LIFE WAS:

....

....

SOMETHING I'VE ALWAYS
FELT PASSIONATE ABOUT IS:

NOTHING HAS INFLUENCED
ME MORE THAN:

....

....

....

THE MOST DIFFICULT DECISION I EVER MADE WAS:

....

....

....

....

....

....

**SOMETHING YOU PROBABLY
DON'T KNOW ABOUT ME IS:**

IF I COULD BE SURE THAT YOU LEARN JUST ONE THING FROM ME, IT WOULD BE:

....

....

....

....

....

....

....

....

IF YOU HAVE ENJOYED USING
AND SHARING THIS BOOK,
WE WOULD LOVE TO HEAR FROM YOU.

Please send your comments to:
Hallmark Book Feedback
P.O. Box 419034
Mail Drop 215
Kansas City, MO 64141

Or e-mail us at:
booknotes@hallmark.com